FOND DU LAC PUBLIC LIBRARY

The 2005
Commemorative

Stamp
Yearbook

UNITED STATES POSTAL SERVICE

Other books available from the United States Postal Service:

THE 2004 COMMEMORATIVE STAMP YEARBOOK

THE POSTAL SERVICE GUIDE TO U.S. STAMPS
32nd Edition

TWA Terminal
NEW YORK, NY USA 37
1962
2005

The 2005 Commemorative
Stamp
Yearbook

37 USA
LOVE
2005

UNITED STATES POSTAL SERVICE

UNITED STATES POSTAL SERVICE

Collins
An Imprint of HarperCollinsPublishers

2005 COMMEMORATIVE STAMP YEARBOOK. Copyright © 2005 by the United States Postal Service.
All rights reserved. Printed in the United States of America. No part of this book may be used or reproduced in
any manner whatsoever without written permission except in the case of brief quotations embodied in critical
articles and reviews. For information address HarperCollins Publishers, 10 East 53rd Street, New York, NY 10022.

The designs of stamps and postal stationery are the subject of individual copyrights by the United States Postal Service.
UNITED STATES POSTAL SERVICE, the eagle logo, and POSTAL SERVICE are trademarks of the United States Postal Service.

HarperCollins books may be purchased for educational, business, or sales promotional use.
For information please write: Special Markets Department, HarperCollins Publishers,
10 East 53rd Street, New York, NY 10022.

Library of Congress Cataloging-in-Publication Data has been applied for.

ISBN-10: 0-06-052824-9
ISBN-13: 978-0-06-052824-9

Contents

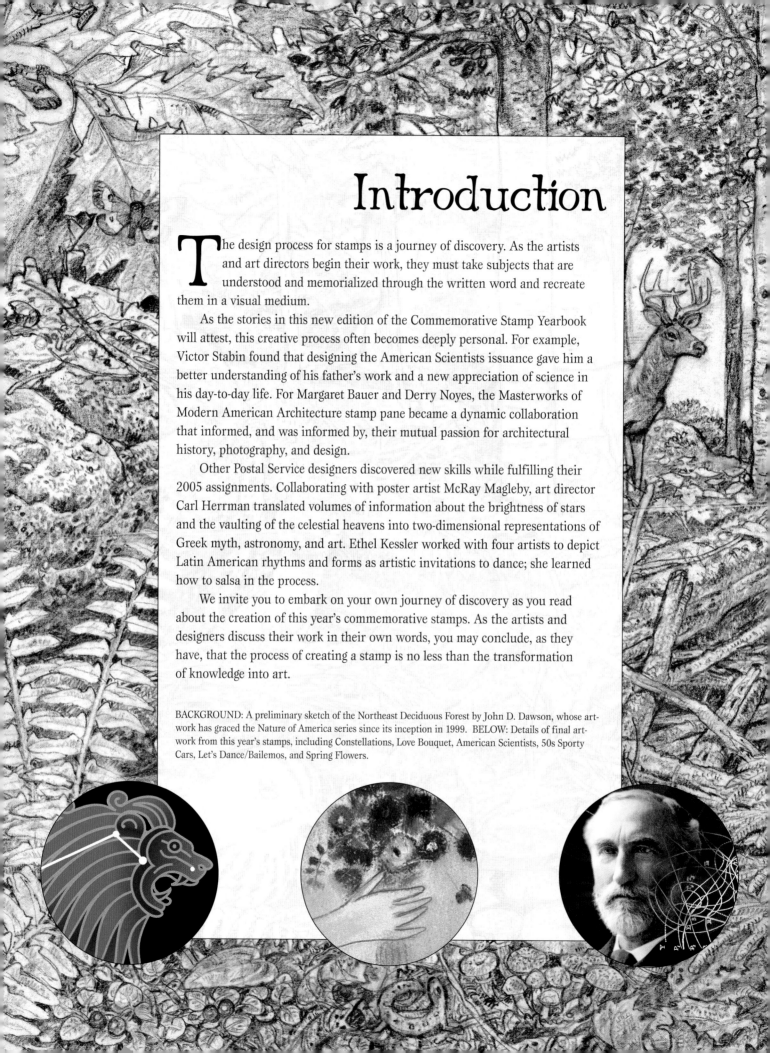

Introduction

The design process for stamps is a journey of discovery. As the artists and art directors begin their work, they must take subjects that are understood and memorialized through the written word and recreate them in a visual medium.

As the stories in this new edition of the Commemorative Stamp Yearbook will attest, this creative process often becomes deeply personal. For example, Victor Stabin found that designing the American Scientists issuance gave him a better understanding of his father's work and a new appreciation of science in his day-to-day life. For Margaret Bauer and Derry Noyes, the Masterworks of Modern American Architecture stamp pane became a dynamic collaboration that informed, and was informed by, their mutual passion for architectural history, photography, and design.

Other Postal Service designers discovered new skills while fulfilling their 2005 assignments. Collaborating with poster artist McRay Magleby, art director Carl Herrman translated volumes of information about the brightness of stars and the vaulting of the celestial heavens into two-dimensional representations of Greek myth, astronomy, and art. Ethel Kessler worked with four artists to depict Latin American rhythms and forms as artistic invitations to dance; she learned how to salsa in the process.

We invite you to embark on your own journey of discovery as you read about the creation of this year's commemorative stamps. As the artists and designers discuss their work in their own words, you may conclude, as they have, that the process of creating a stamp is no less than the transformation of knowledge into art.

BACKGROUND: A preliminary sketch of the Northeast Deciduous Forest by John D. Dawson, whose artwork has graced the Nature of America series since its inception in 1999. BELOW: Details of final artwork from this year's stamps, including Constellations, Love Bouquet, American Scientists, 50s Sporty Cars, Let's Dance/Bailemos, and Spring Flowers.

HAPPY · NEW · YEAR!

恭賀新禧

© 2004 USPS

Lunar New Year Souvenir Sheet

I n 2005, the Lunar New Year stamp series came full circle. Fittingly, the Postal Service celebrated the successful completion of this wildly popular series with a reprinting of all twelve designs on a single pane of stamps.

Terry McCaffrey, art director on the series, worked with Clarence Lee on all twelve designs.

"It was gratifying to conclude by presenting the series as a complete work of art," McCaffrey says. "Over the years, people have asked why we used the less traditional blue and purple backgrounds. Now, when you see them all together, the designs really look terrific."

The Lunar New Year is celebrated by people from Korea, Mongolia, Vietnam, China, and Tibet.

When the complete souvenir sheet was presented to U.S. Postal Service management, a new concern arose, one that had never occurred either to McCaffrey or to Lee, an American of Chinese descent. The face value of the entire sheet was $4.44, a number that can symbolize bad luck in Asian culture. Fortunately, McCaffrey realized that a double-sided self-adhesive sheet would sell for $8.88— a number that symbolizes very good fortune indeed.

Many other postal authorities have issued Lunar New Year stamps, including Canada, South Africa, Hong Kong, and Taiwan, but Lee feels that his designs are unique in their combination of Asian tradition with a modern American visual style. He also hopes that the Postal Service will continue to issue stamps that appeal to Asian Americans.

"When we started this project, the Postal Service didn't have any idea how popular it would be," he says. "But there are 20 million stamp collectors in China alone. And the Lunar New Year is celebrated by people from Korea, Mongolia, Vietnam, and Tibet."

Lee adds that his work on this project has given him a common, if unexpected, bond with people around the world.

"It's wonderful," he says. "Wherever I go, people always ask me about stamps."

PLACE AND DATE OF ISSUE
Honolulu, HI, January 6, 2005

ART DIRECTOR
Terrence W. McCaffrey

DESIGNER AND ARTIST
Clarence Lee

Marian Anderson

"**D**esigning the Marian Anderson stamp was one of the easiest assignments I've ever had," remembers Dick Sheaff, art director for the project. "The University of Pennsylvania has her papers, which include hundreds of photographs. I had never realized how beautiful she was."

Well aware of the iconic moments in Anderson's career, Sheaff further researched Anderson's life with the goal of discovering a unique way to depict the legendary singer.

"At first I thought about using a picture of her when she sang at the Lincoln Memorial during the 1963 March on Washington, because I wanted to show how political she had become and how important she was in the struggle for civil rights," he says. "But as I learned more about her and realized how much of her life she had devoted to developing her musical career, I decided to show the young diva instead."

Sheaff selected a formal black-and-white photographic portrait of Anderson taken in Sweden during the 1930s, when her time abroad was immensely important to her emotional and artistic growth. Confident that he had chosen the perfect photograph, Sheaff then sought out artist Albert Slark to render it as a full-color portrait.

"I spent about two weeks working on the portrait," Slark says. "The hardest part was getting the eyes and the smile just right. I also went to the library to find color photographs of Anderson so I could match the skin tones. I really had fun with it."

Sheaff hopes that the enthusiasm he and Slark brought to this project will be evident to stamp buyers in 2005.

"I wanted this stamp to be an inspiration to all artists of all colors to follow their dream, no matter what it takes," he concludes. "Marian Anderson's musical legacy is a proud one. In some ways, she herself is even more important to us now than ever before."

> *"I wanted this stamp to be an inspiration to all artists of all colors to follow their dream, no matter what it takes."*

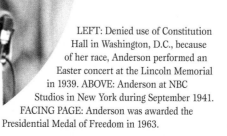

LEFT: Denied use of Constitution Hall in Washington, D.C., because of her race, Anderson performed an Easter concert at the Lincoln Memorial in 1939. ABOVE: Anderson at NBC Studios in New York during September 1941. FACING PAGE: Anderson was awarded the Presidential Medal of Freedom in 1963.

PLACE AND DATE OF ISSUE
Washington, DC, January 27, 2005

ART DIRECTOR AND DESIGNER
Richard Sheaff

ARTIST
Albert Slark

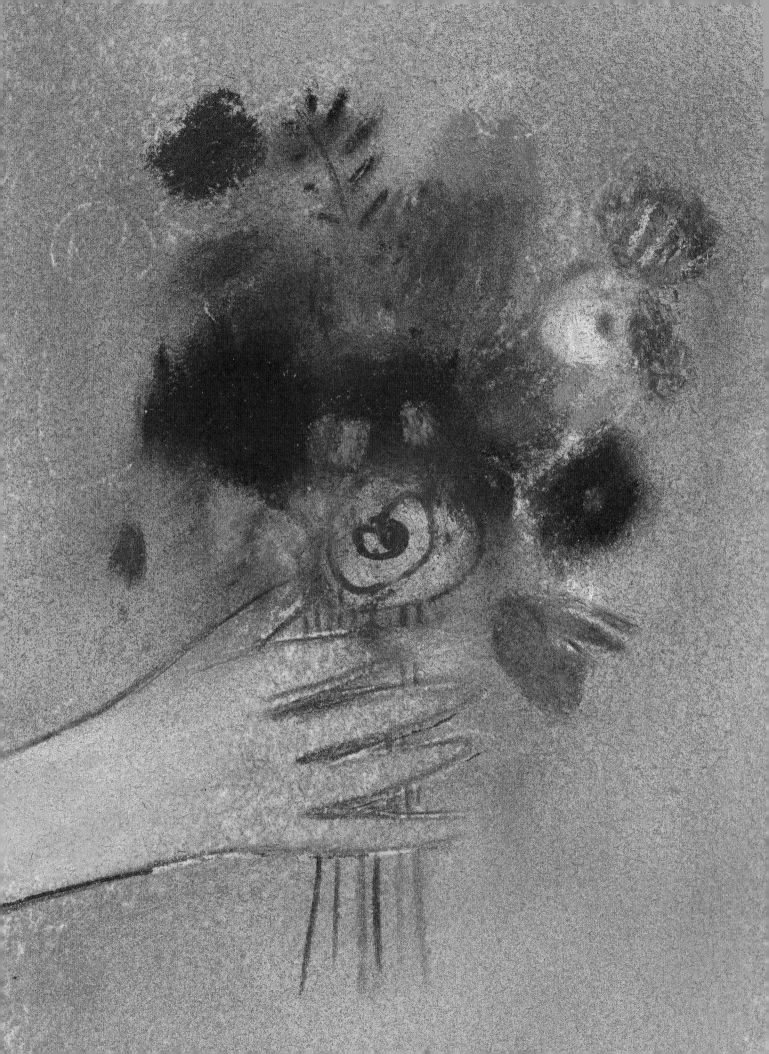

Love Bouquet

"Whenever I'm assigned a new Love stamp, the first thing I think about is the artist," says art director Derry Noyes. "With Vivienne Flesher, I knew right away that her pastels would be perfect. Her work is so vibrant and joyful; it makes you think of love."

Reconceiving approaches to the concept of love is one of the most difficult tasks that Postal Service art directors face. Noyes points out that she first approached Flesher almost 25 years ago about creating a Love stamp, but when she called her last year, she had a specific assignment in mind.

Reconceiving approaches to the concept of love is one of the most difficult tasks that Postal Service art directors face.

"Derry had been working with some beautiful paintings of flowers by the Old Masters," recalls Flesher. "She wanted me to come up with something just as flowery and as beautiful, but much warmer and softer. I immediately thought of the Picasso painting with the hand and the flowers, so I photographed a bunch of kids holding bouquets of daisies and other wildflowers.

"I even photographed my dog sniffing flowers," she admits with a laugh. "Well, I love my dog."

Thinking that she was completing only the first stage of a lengthy process, Flesher sketched a variety of concepts based on her photos. "I was so surprised when Derry called to say that the Postal Service loved two of the sketches," she says. "I had planned to do finished versions of anything they were interested in, but Derry felt that they were perfect just the way they were."

The Love Bouquet will be Vivienne Flesher's first U.S. postage stamp, but it definitely will not be her last. She has another Love design in the works, and she has begun working with Noyes on a new social awareness stamp. Through her work with the Postal Service, Flesher has discovered that designing stamps requires not only a new sense of scale but also a new artistic mindset, one that informs her current Love design above all.

"A work can look so different at stamp size," she concludes. "The original always needs to be clean and calm."

PLACE AND DATE OF ISSUE
Atlanta, GA, February 18, 2005

ART DIRECTOR AND DESIGNER
Derry Noyes

ARTIST
Vivienne Flesher

FACING PAGE: Vivienne Flesher's stamp art inspires generosity and reflection.
ABOVE LEFT: Flowers often warm the heart of a loved one.

Ronald Reagan

Ronald Reagan was sworn in as the 40th president of the United States on January 20, 1981, and served two terms in office. Known as the "Great Communicator," he was adept at advocating his conservative agenda at home, while abroad he promoted a foreign policy that he characterized as "peace through strength."

Regarded as one of the most popular presidents of the 20th century, Reagan inspired the American people, and the Postal Service wanted this stamp to reflect the way in which he renewed Americans' confidence in the nation and its role in the world. "We wanted to create a stamp design that would capture that patriotism, optimism, and charm," explains art director Howard Paine.

The stamp team worked closely with former First Lady Nancy Reagan and the Reagan Foundation to find just the right reference image: a 1981 portrait by White House photographer Jack Kightlinger. "Reagan's features appear so well defined and so chiseled in that photograph it was almost effortless to paint him," says stamp artist Michael J. Deas. "The credit really goes to the photographer.

"I used a dark background for the painting because it made him seem more statesmanlike and timeless," Deas continues. "Usually I try to place something symbolic in the background of a portrait, but President Reagan's life and achievements speak for themselves."

When Paine saw the finished artwork, he liked the contrast between the light on Reagan's face and the darker background. To him the total effect seems symbolic of two of President Reagan's key traits: his confident optimism and his serious yet personable nature. "Michael really did capture Reagan's infectious smile," he says, "the twinkle in his eye, and his ruddy California complexion, as well as his fierce determination and grit."

"We wanted to create a stamp design that would capture that patriotism, optimism, and charm."

LEFT: Ronald and Nancy Reagan greet crowds during his first inauguration in January 1981. ABOVE: The Reagans met in 1951 and remained inseparable for more than 50 years. FACING PAGE: President Reagan relaxes at the White House in 1984.

PLACE AND DATE OF ISSUE
Simi Valley, CA, February 9, 2005

ART DIRECTOR AND DESIGNER
Howard E. Paine

ARTIST
Michael J. Deas

Reagan

Jim Henson: The Man Behind the Muppets

As a director, producer, writer, and puppeteer, Jim Henson is considered one of the most influential artists and entertainers of the 20th century, and his creations continue to delight children and adults alike. The Postal Service celebrates his legacy in 2005 with eleven new postage stamps that coincide with a particularly happy event in Muppet history: the 50th anniversary of the television debut of Kermit the Frog.

Henson design director Edward Eyth envisioned a pane of stamps featuring thirteen of the classic Muppets and a separate stamp to pay tribute to Henson himself.

"When used as postage, we wanted each stamp to provide a colorful, animated, three-dimensional look," Eyth says, "as if the Muppets themselves had burst through the corner of the envelope."

For the final design, Eyth worked with veteran *Rolling Stone* cameraman and Muppet photographer Jay David Buchsbaum.

"Ed and the Henson Creature Shop crew built the set for the photo shoot," explains Buchsbaum, "and we posed the characters in the opening. We had a stylist who had worked with the puppets for years and it still took about an hour to get each one into position. The Muppets are different sizes, so they didn't all fit inside the paper burst."

To make sure that the photographs were going to work at stamp size, Buchsbaum created an acetate overlay that could be positioned over the viewfinder to indicate what the final composition would look like, including the puppet's location relative to the 37-cent denomination. He explains that working with Muppets can be as challenging as a shoot with live subjects—although in this case, for specifically stamp-related reasons.

"We'd get the puppet all set up, and then we'd run back to the camera and find out that we'd covered the 37-cent sign," he says with a laugh. "It took us all day to get it right."

> *"We wanted each stamp to provide a colorful, animated, three-dimensional look, as if the Muppets themselves had burst through the corner of the envelope."*

PLACE AND DATE OF ISSUE
Los Angeles, CA, September 28, 2005

ART DIRECTOR
Terrence W. McCaffrey

DESIGNER
Edward Eyth

PHOTOGRAPHER
Jay David Buchsbaum

FACING PAGE: Henson poses with his Muppet friends in 1978. ABOVE: Henson began his career as a puppeteer on a children's television program in Washington, D.C.

Spring Flowers

When art director Derry Noyes contacted Chris Pullman to ask whether he and his wife Esther, past president of the Cambridge Plant and Garden Club, would be interested in designing stamps featuring spring flowers, they were extremely enthusiastic—despite certain seasonal limitations.

"We started working on this project in the dead of winter, and the selection of fresh flowers was very limited," remembers Pullman. "Most of the early spring flowers that were available were bulbs, so that became the organizing idea for these stamps."

However, once they got started, a number of other ideas emerged. "With all the beautiful flowers in the house and the images we produced in the studio and found during our research, we were tempted to try other approaches," Pullman explains. "For example, we thought about the idea of tiny flowers that could be reproduced actual size on the stamps. We also collected many beautiful eighteenth- and nineteenth-century botanical illustrations, which would have given the set a more historical feel."

In the end, Noyes presented seven different variations to the Citizens' Stamp Advisory Committee, which selected a hand-painted design by Christopher Pullman—much to the surprise of Pullman himself. "I've painted watercolors for many years," he says, "but I had almost never used any of these paintings in my professional work."

Once the decision was made to use watercolors, the design progressed quickly. Within the year, Pullman had completed several paintings, which Noyes predicts will make these stamps extremely popular.

"They're very different from flower stamps that the Postal Service has issued in the past," she says. "As silhouettes on white backgrounds, Chris Pullman's watercolors are striking in their clean simplicity. I'm sure that people will be glad to use them for weddings, love letters, and virtually any other happy occasion."

"We also collected many beautiful eighteenth- and nineteenth-century botanical illustrations, which would have given the set a more historical feel."

LEFT and ABOVE: Christopher Pullman's watercolors bring a splash of springtime color to this attractive new issuance.

PLACE AND DATE OF ISSUE
Chicago, IL, March 15, 2005

ART DIRECTOR
Derry Noyes

DESIGNER AND ARTIST
Christopher Pullman

Northeast Deciduous Forest

Now on his seventh design in the Nature of America series, John D. Dawson admits that the Northeast Deciduous Forest was one of the harder stamp panes to create. Deciding to experiment, he started sketching the scene with a view from the beaver pond looking out.

"I think everyone who saw that early sketch quickly realized that it wasn't the best perspective," he says ruefully, "so we decided to move up the hill and look down at the pond. After that change, the work moved along smoothly."

The deciduous forests of the northeastern United States are identified by trees that shed their leaves. Even though Dawson lives in Hilo, Hawaii, he owns numerous boxes of leaves, leaf litter, and varied assortments of ground debris collected from his travels to all corners of the United States.

"To create the scene, I lay out my guidebooks, photographs, field sketches, notes, and all 'debris reference materials' that I have personally gathered," he explains. "Then I begin sketching."

After Dawson creates a detailed pencil sketch, he shares his work with scientists whose expertise is in the plant and animal life of the region.

"Depicting the right relationships between organisms is a balancing act unless you are actually in the field and painting directly from nature," he says. "I rely on the experts, as well as the art director, to tell me if anything in the scene is not completely accurate in size, scale, proportion, et cetera."

Ethel Kessler, the art director who has worked with Dawson on every Nature of America pane, finds the behind-the-scenes research as important as the development of the art itself.

"We designed these stamps to make people appreciate the flora and fauna of the United States, so they have to be true to life," she says. "Working with John on these stamps is always a pleasure—and each new pane is an adventure."

"We designed these stamps to make people appreciate the flora and fauna of the United States, so they have to be true to life."

PLACE AND DATE OF ISSUE
New York, NY, March 3, 2005

ART DIRECTOR AND DESIGNER
Ethel Kessler

ARTIST
John D. Dawson

McClintock

Gibbs

von Neumann

Feynman

American Scientists

"My only regret about doing this project," says Victor Stabin, the artist for the American Scientists stamps, "is that my father didn't live to see it. He worked at Oak Ridge National Laboratory building scientific instrumentation. The whole time I was designing these stamps, I thought about how great it is that the Postal Service is honoring people who work in the sciences."

For this 2005 issuance, the Postal Service brings together four extraordinary individuals: Barbara McClintock, who discovered genetic transposition; John von Neumann, who made significant contributions in both pure and applied mathematics; Richard Feynman, who developed a new formulation of quantum theory; and Josiah Willard Gibbs, who formulated the modern system of thermodynamic analysis.

In designing these stamps, Stabin wanted to convey the complexity of each individual's achievements. For the Feynman design, he struggled with how to show the physicist's multiple roles as teacher, amateur artist, and Nobel Prize winner. Shown in the background of the stamp are representations of innovative diagrams Feynman created to help visualize the dynamics of atomic particles. For Gibbs, there were very few photographs available; the portrait selected was taken toward the end of Gibbs's life. The background diagram was created much later as an interpretation of his work.

John von Neumann is perhaps best remembered for his work with computers in the 1940s and early 1950s. "For von Neumann," Stabin says, "I wanted the background to relate in some way to this early work; we searched for a long time before finding rough notes from one of his first computer programs." For the McClintock design, Stabin paired a 1983 portrait with a diagram from the 1940s. McClintock's first recognition of genetic transposition was captured in this figure showing chromosome breaks.

Given his family background, Stabin hopes the American Scientists stamps will ignite newfound interest in the lives and careers of these four brilliant figures.

"If people look at these stamps and become curious about who these people were, it will create an opportunity for Americans to learn about science and to discuss the amazing work these individuals conducted," he says. "That makes it all worthwhile."

> *"I thought about how great it is that the Postal Service is honoring people who work in the sciences."*

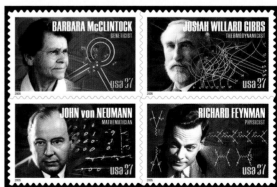

PLACE AND DATE OF ISSUE
New Haven, CT, May 4, 2005

ART DIRECTOR
Carl T. Herrman

DESIGNER
Victor Stabin

FACING PAGE: Barbara McClintock speaks in 1983 after learning that she will receive the Nobel Prize for Medicine. Some historians and scientists have declared the discoveries of Josiah Willard Gibbs to be as fundamental in nature as those of Galileo and Newton. John von Neumann's contributions to mathematics included a machine that became a model for virtually all modern computers. Richard P. Feynman was a highly original theoretical physicist and an inspiring teacher—as well as an amateur artist and bongo drummer. ABOVE: Feynman's blackboard at the time of his death in 1988.

Robert Penn Warren

When the time came to create this stamp honoring the nation's first official poet laureate, Carl Herrman was faced with a challenge that confronts every art director who begins a new Literary Arts issuance.

"We're always looking for portrait artists who can paint good human likenesses as well as backgrounds," Herrman explains. "The format of the Literary Arts series is not an easy one. Just because an artist can illustrate faces doesn't mean that he or she can paint landscapes."

Fortunately, Herrman had his eye on an artist who had demonstrated an ability to "work small," a vital skill in the world of stamp design.

"Although Will Wilson had never done a stamp, I trusted him absolutely," he explains. "I had seen his painting of mice playing instruments. It was only seven inches wide, but you could almost count every hair."

Wilson was pleased by the amount of freedom he was given, but he approached this project knowing that his artwork needed to be built around one specific element.

"I knew that there was really only one photograph that would work," he says. "It was a fairly stiff black-and-white portrait taken around the time Warren published *All the King's Men*."

To Herrman, complementing the portrait with a background scene from the novel made perfect sense. "Will gave us three sketches using different elements in the background," he says, "but *All the King's Men* was the hook. It had to be. Robert Penn Warren was a Southern writer, and that's a quintessentially Southern novel."

A distinguished man of letters, Warren won the Pulitzer Prize three times, and he remains the only writer so far to have won the prize in poetry—in 1958 and again in 1979—as well as in fiction. Herrman expresses satisfaction at Wilson's ability to capture the essence of this complex American writer.

"Somehow he has imbued the stamp art with a Depression-era feel," Herrman says. "It has a 1930s look that adds something special to the overall design. Just as Robert Penn Warren was a master of prose and poetry, Will Wilson really knows how to tell a story through art."

ABOVE: Warren revises a textbook inside the barn where he wrote. FACING PAGE: Warren was America's first official poet laureate and a three-time recipient of the Pulitzer Prize. INSET: The cover of the first edition of *All the King's Men*, published in 1947.

A distinguished man of letters, Warren won the Pulitzer Prize three times, and he remains the only writer so far to have won the prize in poetry as well as in fiction.

PLACE AND DATE OF ISSUE
Guthrie, KY, April 22, 2005

ART DIRECTOR AND DESIGNER
Carl T. Herrman

ARTIST
Will Wilson

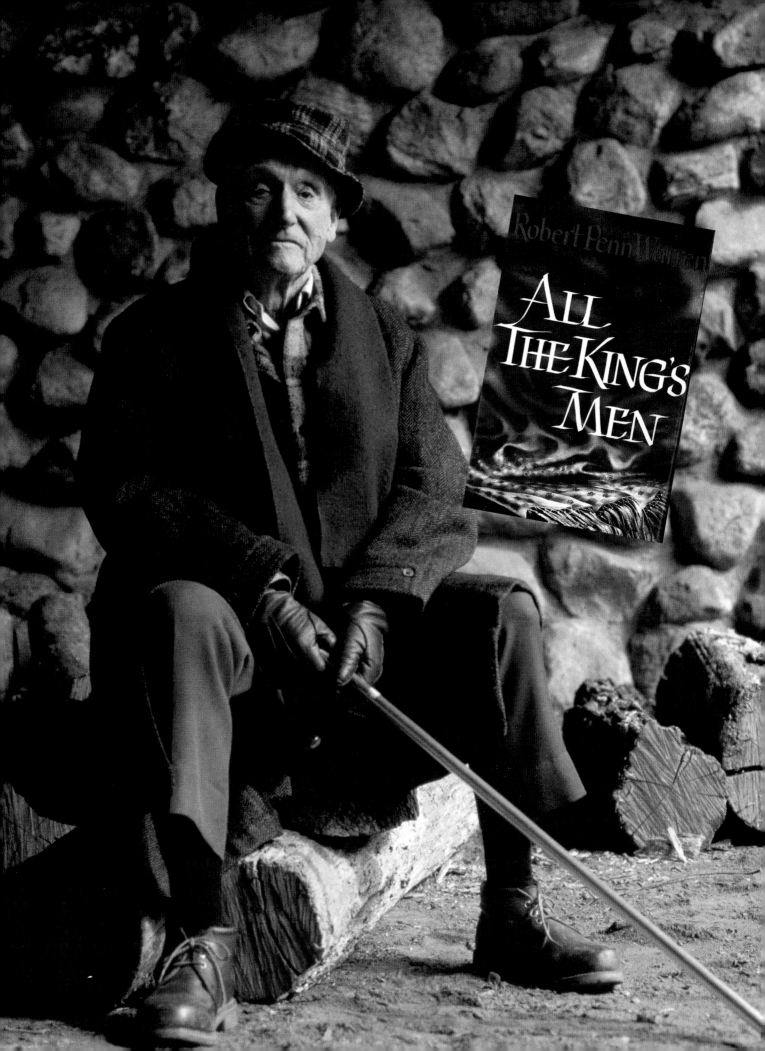

Yip Harburg

"I've photographed a lot of famous people, but when you'd walk into a room with Yip Harburg, people would stand and applaud," remembers photographer Barbara Bordnick. The photograph of the famous songster shown on this stamp was originally an eight-by-ten Polaroid, a new medium when Bordnick shot the photo in 1978.

Harburg's work was distinguished by his intelligence, inventiveness, and humanity. He supplied the lyrics for several standards, including "Over the Rainbow," "April in Paris," and "Brother, Can You Spare a Dime?" After he was blacklisted in Hollywood in the 1950s due to his political views, Harburg concentrated on writing for the Broadway stage. In addition to penning the lyrics for more than 600 popular songs, he is credited with helping to transform the musical play from a star vehicle into a story in which music and dance advance the plot rather than interrupt it.

"We worked together for two hours," says Bordnick, remembering the time she spent photographing the master lyricist. "I told him my mother had sung his 'How Are Things in Glocca Morra?' to me as a child and he started to talk to me about his music. He even sang to me. He was so genuine, warm, and imaginative—and wonderfully mischievous."

For Ethel Kessler, art director on the project, including the lyrics and the rainbow added a special poignancy to the stamp design. In 1939, when Harburg was at work on *The Wizard of Oz*, there was preliminary talk of cutting "Over the Rainbow" from the finished film. Eventually, of course, the song won an Oscar, and today many consider it the top song of the 20th century.

"He was so genuine, warm, and imaginative— and wonderfully mischievous."

"The photograph of Yip makes the stamp," Kessler says. "We considered earlier photographs of him in Hollywood, but in this photograph Barbara really captured something very special about the man. What's amazing is that he's 82 years old in the photo. You can just feel his love of life."

PLACE AND DATE OF ISSUE
New York, NY, April 28, 2005

ART DIRECTOR AND DESIGNER
Ethel Kessler

PHOTOGRAPHER
Barbara Bordnick

FACING PAGE: In this 1978 photograph, Harburg sings "Over the Rainbow" to photographer Barbara Bordnick. INSET: Sheet music from *Finian's Rainbow* and *The Wizard of Oz*, both featuring lyrics by Harburg. ABOVE: This portrait appeared on the cover of the album "Yip Sings Harburg."

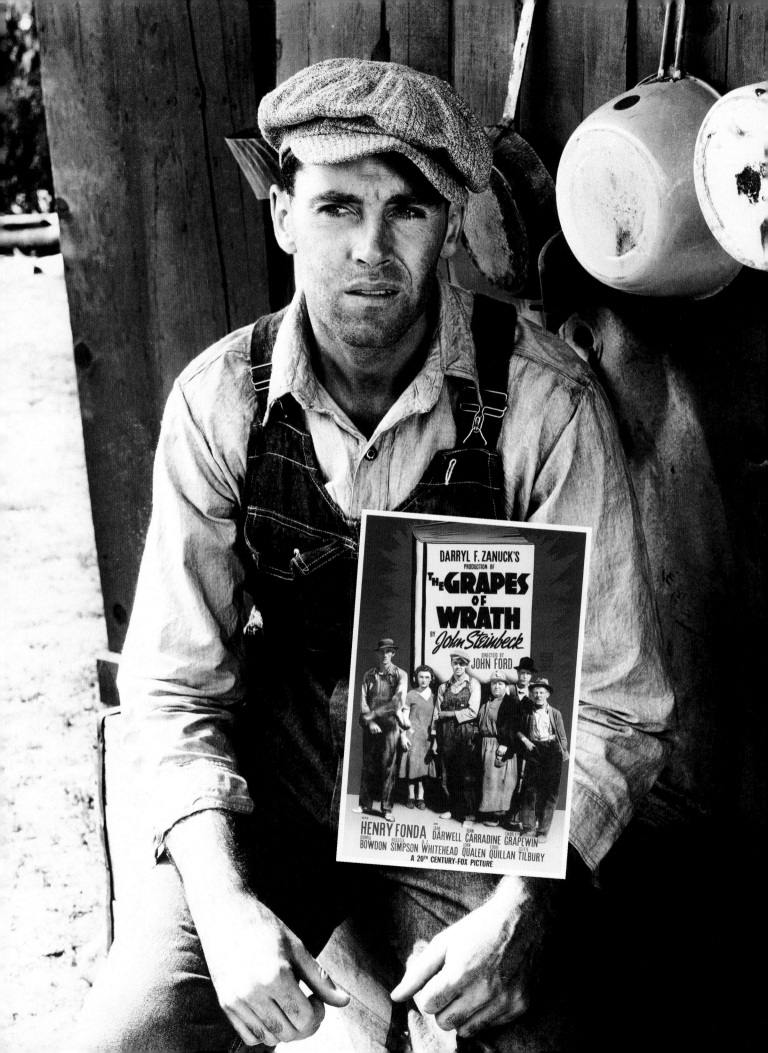

Henry Fonda

Legends of Hollywood

enry Fonda received many honors during his lifetime, including a Tony Award in 1948 for the Broadway comedy *Mister Roberts* and an Oscar in 1982 for his role in the film *On Golden Pond*. He was also honored in 1981 with a special Academy Award for his contribution to film, and in 1979 he was the recipient of a special Tony for his work in the American theater. This year, the Postal Service continues to recognize Fonda with a commemorative stamp issued on the 100th anniversary of his birth.

"The hardest part of this assignment was finding one or two images that conveyed Henry Fonda's range as an actor," notes art director Derry Noyes. After all, Fonda was a versatile performer who was equally effective in comedic and dramatic roles; he claimed it was therapeutic to pretend to be someone else.

For the portrait, the Postal Service turned to Drew Struzan, an artist internationally recognized for his work on movie posters. Struzan has also established himself as one of the leading stamp artists, having created artwork for many issuances in the Legends of Hollywood series—including, most recently, John Wayne.

Struzan based the portrait on a studio photograph shot by Frank Powolny in 1941. "I wanted to get a very smooth, finished look for the young Henry Fonda," he says. "I was trying to capture the look of the man of integrity; that's the role he so often played."

For the selvage, Noyes wanted to use a distinctive image from *The Grapes of Wrath*.

"Fonda's portrayal of Tom Joad was so powerful," she says. "I wanted the illustration to have a larger-than-life quality. Drew's sketch had a spontaneity and gutsiness to it that worked perfectly in contrast to the portrait."

"The *Grapes of Wrath* art is much rougher," Struzan adds. "I tried to match the emotion of the movie and the roughness of the masculine character. I like the combination of the two. The refined character of the portrait and the roughness of the selvage really work together beautifully."

"I was trying to capture the look of the man of integrity; that's the role he so often played."

FACING PAGE: Fonda portrayed Tom Joad in the acclaimed 1940 motion picture *The Grapes of Wrath*. ABOVE: A reflective Fonda, circa 1960. RIGHT: Fonda appeared with Katharine Hepburn in his final film, *On Golden Pond*.

PLACE AND DATE OF ISSUE
Beverly Hills, CA, May 20, 2005

ART DIRECTOR AND DESIGNER
Derry Noyes

ARTIST
Drew Struzan

Distinguished Marines

With the issuance of the Distinguished Marines stamps, the U.S. Postal Service honors four legendary leathernecks who served with bravery and distinction during the 20th century: John Basilone, Daniel J. Daly, John A. Lejeune, and Lewis B. Puller.

"It wasn't difficult to select the individuals on this sheet," reports Phil Jordan, the art director for these stamps. "They volunteered themselves by their exemplary service to our country. The difficulty was limiting the sheet to four. Four dozen would have been better—but even then not all-inclusive." Jordan felt unusually qualified for the assignment: His father was a Navy Seabee attached to the First Marine Division in World War II, and he grew up in New Bern, North Carolina, right in the middle of the Second Marine Division.

Designed to complement the Distinguished Soldiers stamp pane issued in 2000, the Distinguished Marines pane features an officer and an enlisted man who served in World War I and another pair who served in World War II. All four men went above and beyond the call of duty and remain Marine Corps icons to this day.

"Researching the history of the Marine Corps, we were witness to many examples of selfless service, devotion, and courage," Jordan says. "These stamps are for a Corps of men and women—past, present, and future—united by the spirit of their universally shared credo: *Semper Fidelis*.

"Whatever you think about war, these guys are the ones who stepped up," Jordan concludes. "They are genuine heroes."

"Researching the history of the Marine Corps, we were witness to many examples of selfless service, devotion, and courage."

LEFT: A group of marines lands on the Normandy coast on D Day, June 6, 1944. CLOCKWISE FROM LEFT: Insignias associated with these marines include the 73rd Machine Gun Company; the 5th Marine Division; the Army's 2nd Infantry Division, which Lejeune commanded during World War I; and the 1st Marine Division. FACING PAGE: Members of the U.S. Marine Corps raise the American flag on Mount Suribachi on February 23, 1945, after the Battle of Iwo Jima.

PLACE AND DATE OF ISSUE
Washington, DC, November 10, 2005

ART DIRECTOR AND DESIGNER
Phil Jordan

**Masterworks of
Modern American
Architecture**

Masterworks of Modern American Architecture

"**W**hen we began this project, everything was big," recalls art director Derry Noyes. "The subject was big, the buildings were big, and we wanted the stamps to be big, too. I think we accomplished that—even though over the course of a year, the project evolved from a prestige booklet with stories and photos about each architect to twelve individual stamps that recognized specific buildings."

The resulting stamp pane honors twelve 20th-century buildings that are considered the finest examples of modern American architecture. Noyes and designer Margaret Bauer are confident that these stamps also represent another worthy accomplishment: a successful collaboration between two professional designers who are passionate about their subject.

"I've always loved architecture," says Bauer, whose stamp design credits include the 2002 Teddy Bears issuance. "Working on this project was a pleasure, because of the subject matter and because Derry and I work so well together as a team. There was a tremendous amount of back and forth, each of us refining what the other one did."

Noyes says that their brainstorming finally paid off when she and Bauer began to focus on individual buildings rather than on a specific architect or historic period. Bauer adds that discovering the work of a master photographer was also a major milestone.

"For me, finding Ezra Stoller's photographs, with their striking architectural details, was what settled the design concept," she says. "I had tried working with black-and-white photos alongside color images, but using both upset the balance. In the end I knew that an entire pane of black-and-white images would do the job beautifully."

"The process is a tremendous amount of work, but if the viewer sees only something that seems elegant and effortless, then we have definitely succeeded at our task."

PLACE AND DATE OF ISSUE
Las Vegas, NV, May 19, 2005

ART DIRECTOR
Derry Noyes

DESIGNER
Margaret Bauer

FACING PAGE: A dizzying view of Ludwig Mies van der Rohe's 860-880 Lake Shore Drive in Chicago. ABOVE RIGHT: Architect Philip Johnson in 2002. LOWER RIGHT: Eero Saarinen, architect of the TWA Terminal, in 1940.

Once Noyes and Bauer had paired the right concept with the right photographs, the design took on a life of its own. After selecting a color palette and typeface, Bauer began the process of scanning and cropping photos of various buildings to determine which images worked not only as individual stamps, but also within the context of the entire stamp pane. She observed that the photographs needed to be compatible but distinctive—a design phenomenon that she describes with an unusual and thoughtful analogy.

"Like a family," she says. "And like a family, they each had to have room. I couldn't have too many angles all together, or too many curves together. The details needed to be separated from each other so that someone who looked at all of the stamps together could tell that they were honoring buildings—whether we showed an interior or exterior shot—but each stamp needed to be able to stand on its own as well."

Despite the many permutations of this project, Noyes and Bauer knew that one "sure thing" had to appear in their finished design: a three-dimensional view of the High Museum of Art in Atlanta, Georgia.

"We did try some sketches and other drawings," Noyes says, "but that background image was the design element that really held the individual stamps together. It sets off the colors of the type beautifully, and it adds a completely different level of structure and organization to the sheet."

In the end, Noyes and Bauer have created a fitting tribute to their stamp subjects, recognizing architectural masterpieces for their beauty and intelligence of design through a stamp pane that shares both of those attributes.

"Despite the differences in scale, the mindsets are similar, whether you're designing a building or creating a pane of stamps," says Noyes. "No matter the size, all design work requires professionalism, an awareness of the big picture, and above all, a willingness to collaborate. The process is a tremendous amount of work, but if the viewer sees only something that seems elegant and effortless, then we have definitely succeeded at our task."

ABOVE LEFT: Frank Lloyd Wright converses with students. ABOVE RIGHT: Louis Kahn, architect of the library at Phillips Exeter Academy. BELOW RIGHT: Architect Paul Rudolph, the mind behind the Yale Art and Architecture Building. FACING PAGE: Walt Disney Concert Hall in Los Angeles, California, designed by Frank Gehry. TOP: Architect I.M. Pei, who designed the East Building of the National Gallery of Art. BOTTOM: Architect Richard Meier, designer of the High Museum of Art in Atlanta, Georgia.

American Advances in Aviation

After the blockbuster success of the 1997 Classic American Aircraft stamp pane, artist William S. Phillips was pleased to learn that there was a groundswell of public support for a follow-up issuance featuring more of his work. In particular, the Postal Service received thousands of letters from World War II veterans who wanted to see the B-29 Superfortress on a stamp before they died. "It was really an all-out effort," recalls Phil Jordan, art director for both projects.

With the insight gained from experience, Phillips found working on the second stamp pane much easier than the first.

"I realized that this time around I would have to produce what amounted to a portrait of each aircraft, rather than the action scenes I usually paint," he says. "The YB-49 Flying Wing was the most challenging and the most fun. I wanted to show the geometric shape of that plane to best advantage so one could really see how 'cutting edge' it was in the late 1940s. I'm really pleased with the way the light reflects off the metal in that painting.

"I carefully selected suitable landscapes to use as backdrops," Phillips continues, "because I wanted the background colors to enhance and complement the portrait of each plane. I also knew that once I finished my paintings, Phil would then do his magic. I think the stamp designs are really superb, especially the way they all work together."

One of the men who petitioned the Postal Service for this second stamp pane flew a B-24 Liberator during World War II. For Jordan and Phillips he exemplified the pilots and crews of these incredible machines. Sadly, he died before the stamp art was completed, but everyone involved with this project acknowledges that it was his enthusiasm, knowledge, and persistence that helped bring the American Advances in Aviation stamp pane to fruition.

"I carefully selected suitable landscapes to use as backdrops because I wanted the background colors to enhance and complement the portrait of each plane."

PLACE AND DATE OF ISSUE
Vienna, VA, and Oshkosh, WI, July 29, 2005

ART DIRECTOR AND DESIGNER
Phil Jordan

ARTIST
William S. Phillips

FACING PAGE: A rendering of the YB-49 Flying Wing by stamp artist William S. Phillips. ABOVE LEFT: A P-80 Shooting Star. ABOVE RIGHT: A 35 Bonanza.

Arthur Ashe

ostal Service designers find perfect art in unexpected places, as Carl Herrman was reminded when he began working on the stamp to commemorate Arthur Ashe, the first African-American man to win Grand Slam tennis tournaments. Herrman happened to be walking through a photo gallery in La Jolla, California, one afternoon when he noticed a striking photograph of Ashe hanging on the wall. He bought the print immediately, and a few days later he contacted the photographer, Michael O'Neill.

O'Neill, who photographed Ashe for the cover of *Sports Illustrated* in 1992, was thrilled at the prospect of his photo being used on a stamp. He told Herrman that he had hoped to capture not only Ashe's athletic side, but also his intellect and integrity.

Because he was black, Ashe was barred from entering competitions in the South, yet his enthusiasm for the sport and the tenacity he developed in his childhood never flagged. A thinker with an insatiable thirst for knowledge, Ashe examined the issues of race, politics, education, and culture in America. In his best-selling memoir *Days of Grace,* he offered an honest assessment of what he had experienced and what he saw happening in American culture. His three-volume work, *A Hard Road to Glory: A History of the African-American Athlete,* required years of original research; a television program based on the book earned him an Emmy.

Ashe's commitment to social issues led him to establish foundations to help disenfranchised young people, to oppose apartheid in South Africa, and to fight AIDS, which he contracted from a blood transfusion following heart surgery. Shortly before his death on February 6, 1993, Ashe spoke before the UN General Assembly and urged countries to increase their efforts to fight the disease.

Herrman remains pleased by how well O'Neill's photograph accurately portrays Ashe's character and spirit. "What makes it so powerful," he says, "is that while you immediately recognize that it's Arthur Ashe because of the tennis racket, what draws you in is his intellect and dignity. You can tell that he's an incredibly positive role model, determined to keep moving forward."

A thinker with an insatiable thirst for knowledge, Ashe examined the issues of race, politics, education, and culture in America.

ABOVE: Ashe dominates the court in 1968. FACING PAGE: Ashe raises his trophy after defeating Jimmy Connors at Wimbledon in 1975. INSET: Ashe's widow, Jeanne Moutoussamy-Ashe, and their daughter, Camera, view the unveiled stamp.

Arthur Ashe™ c/o CMG Worldwide, Indianapolis, IN

PLACE AND DATE OF ISSUE
Flushing Meadow, NY
August 27, 2005

ART DIRECTOR AND DESIGNER
Carl T. Herrman

PHOTOGRAPHER
Michael O'Neill

Arthur Ashe

The Art of Disney: Celebration

When Terrence W. McCaffrey, art director and manager of Stamp Development, Stamp Services, began working with the creative team at Disney to consider which themes the Postal Service should celebrate on these long-awaited Disney commemoratives, they quickly realized that one idea deserved particular consideration: the idea of celebration itself.

"Featuring 'celebration' as one of the themes of this series made perfect sense," McCaffrey says. "Stamps help spread the word about a wide range of celebrations, including anniversaries, birthdays, you name it. With all of the characters in the Disney pantheon and the nearly infinite number of ways to depict them, we were sure we could make the concept work."

Disney fans have long hoped to see U.S. commemoratives featuring some of their favorite characters, and McCaffrey is confident that these stamps will not disappoint.

"A collaboration between the U.S. Postal Service and Disney was a natural pairing," he says. "Disney characters have such wide appeal not only in the United States but also worldwide, and there's something quintessentially American about them. By featuring icons such as Mickey Mouse on our stamps, our commemorative program continues to represent some of our favorite cultural creations."

Pleased with the final stamp artwork, McCaffrey points to the joint creative efforts of artist Peter Emmerich and creative director David Pacheco as a key reason for the success of these designs.

"Both David's creative concepts and Peter's artwork capture the essence of these characters," McCaffrey says. "They both have considerable experience as Disney artists, and they know just what Disney fans are looking for."

When he considers this three-issuance Disney series as a whole, McCaffrey concludes that the public is sure to be satisfied by these lively and heartwarming stamps.

"When we commemorate friendship, celebration, and romance, we're dealing with universal concepts," he says. "People respond positively to that."

> *"A collaboration between the U.S. Postal Service and Disney was a natural pairing."*

PLACE AND DATE OF ISSUE
Anaheim, CA, June 30, 2005

ART DIRECTOR
Terrence W. McCaffrey

DESIGNER
David Pacheco

ILLUSTRATOR
Peter Emmerich

Disney Materials © Disney

New Mexico Rio Grande Blankets

Since its inception in 2001, the American Treasures series has offered several small but exquisite lessons in art and visual culture. This year's issuance features a particularly beautiful Southwestern tradition: textiles produced in colonial Spanish settlements in the northern Rio Grande Valley.

"They were influenced by Spanish, Mexican, Pueblo, and Navajo designs," says art director Derry Noyes, who chose the four 19th-century New Mexico Rio Grande blankets shown on these stamps. "When you study the art form, you also learn the history of the region."

Spanish immigrants began colonizing the Rio Grande Valley in 1598, bringing the churro sheep. Later immigrants brought the horizontal treadle loom. Some families set up looms in their homes; others established organized weaving workshops and used Spanish and Indian labor until the Pueblo Revolt of 1680. After the Spanish regained control of New Mexico in 1692, the Hispanic weaving industry resumed in a more cooperative fashion and thrived throughout the 18th century and the better part of the 19th century.

The synthetic-dyed red, orange, yellow, and white blanket—owned by the Taylor Museum in Colorado Springs—features the traditional Rio Grande band and stripe pattern derived from the striped designs of earlier Pueblo cotton textiles. The Museum of New Mexico in Santa Fe owns the other three blankets. One shows a large central serrate diamond on a complex background, which is representative of the Mexican Saltillo serape designs taught to Rio Grande weavers in the early 19th century. Another combines the band and stripe pattern with small Saltillo-style serrate diamonds and stepped chevrons. The design of the indigo-dyed blanket, with stepped chevrons forming diamonds at the center seam, is related to the Navajo chief blanket.

"From an aesthetic point of view," Noyes says, "I wanted a variety of blanket patterns and colors, but they also had to work together as stamp designs. I also wanted to convey a sense of skill and craftsmanship. That's the best way to pay tribute not only to this centuries-old tradition, but also to the weavers who are keeping it alive today."

"From an aesthetic point of view, I wanted a variety of blanket patterns and colors, but they also had to work together as stamp designs."

LEFT: Mr. and Mrs Esquipula Martínez, Plaza del Cerro, ca. 1910. Mrs. Martínez is preparing a skein of wool using the skein winder attached to the loom. ABOVE: Ramoncita Martinez and Tomasita Martinez are carding and spinning with a malacate or supported spindle. FACING PAGE: The large blanket was woven in the Rio Grande saltillo style, derived from the serapes of Saltillo, Mexico.

PLACE AND DATE OF ISSUE
Santa Fe, NM, July 30, 2005

ART DIRECTOR AND DESIGNER
Derry Noyes

TO FORM A MORE PERFECT UNION

SEEKING EQUAL RIGHTS FOR AFRICAN AMERICANS

1948 Executive Order 9981   37 USA

1960 Lunch Counter Sit-Ins   37 USA

1955 Montgomery Bus Boycott   37 USA

1964 Civil Rights Act   37 USA

"FOR IN A REAL SENSE,
AMERICA IS ESSENTIALLY A DREAM,
A DREAM AS YET UNFULFILLED.
IT IS A DREAM OF A LAND WHERE MEN
OF ALL RACES, OF ALL NATIONALITIES
AND OF ALL CREEDS CAN LIVE
TOGETHER AS BROTHERS."

MARTIN LUTHER KING, JR.

1963 March on Washington   37 USA

1965 Selma March   37 USA

1965 Voting Rights Act   37 USA

1957 Little Rock Nine   37 USA

1961 Freedom Riders   37 USA

1954 Brown v. Board of Education   37 USA

To Form a More Perfect Union

The title selected by the Postal Service for this stamp pane issued in 2005 to celebrate the African-American civil rights movement comes from the opening sentence of the U.S. Constitution:

We the people of the United States, in order to form a more perfect union, establish justice, insure domestic tranquility, provide for the common defense, promote the general welfare, and secure the blessings of liberty to ourselves and our posterity, do ordain and establish this Constitution for the United States of America.

The stamps commemorate ten milestone events in the civil rights movement and honor the courage of countless individuals who changed this country for the better.

"I was inspired by the Smithsonian exhibition 'In the Spirit of Martin: The Living Legacy of Dr. Martin Luther King, Jr.,'" recalls art director Ethel Kessler. "The works in the show made me want to know more about the history and more about the artists. I wanted to use artwork in the same way for the stamps: to make them a message of hope, something personal and uplifting."

Working with Richard Powell, chairman of the art and art history department at Duke University, the design team identified relevant works by ten artists, the majority of them African-American. For example, *Walking* by Charles Alston shows the determination and spirit of the men and women who boycotted the Montgomery bus system. Alma Thomas, considered a genius of color and form, participated in the March on Washington in 1963; she completed the painting *March on Washington* in 1964. In 1984, the NAACP selected Romare Bearden's lithograph *The Lamp* to be on a poster celebrating the 30th anniversary of the *Brown v. Board of Education* decision in 1954. *America Cares,*

> *The stamps commemorate ten milestone events in the civil rights movement and honor the courage of countless individuals who changed this country for the better.*

PLACE AND DATE OF ISSUE

Greensboro, NC, Jackson, MS, Little Rock, AR, Memphis, TN, Montgomery, AL, Selma, AL, Topeka, KS, Washington DC, August 30, 2005

ART DIRECTOR AND DESIGNER

Ethel Kessler

FACING PAGE: In this iconic scene, crowds gather during the March on Washington on August 28, 1963. ABOVE LEFT: A high school student in Clinton, Tennessee, in 1956 during the early days of integration. ABOVE RIGHT: President Johnson signs the Civil Rights Bill into law on July 2, 1964.

The name, likeness, and copyrighted words of Dr. Martin Luther King, Jr., are used by permission of Intellectual Properties Management, Atlanta, Georgia, as exclusive licensor of the King estate.

a portrait of the Little Rock Nine by George Hunt, was commissioned in 1997 to honor the integration of Central High School in Little Rock, Arkansas.

"It was difficult to find works that responded to, or commented on, Executive Order 9981, the Civil Rights Act of 1964, or the Voting Rights Act of 1965," Kessler says. "Dr. Powell suggested that we look at William H. Johnson's 1942 series on the Army. The painting we selected, *Training for War*, doesn't show the effect of President Truman's decision to integrate the military, but it speaks powerfully about the segregation that existed.

Kessler says that the design team hoped to bring together different artistic styles and mediums to make them work together as a whole.

"Each may be powerful on its own," she says, "but they are all even more effective as parts of a larger design. We used everything: lithographs, oil paintings, gouaches, sculpture, and black-and-white photographs. We used works by well-known artists and by artists we had never heard of. That diversity was important. The whole time we were working, we stayed focused on Dr. King's dream."

LEFT: Elizabeth Eckford, one of nine black students admitted to Central High School in Little Rock, Arkansas, by the order of a federal court in September 1967. ABOVE RIGHT: Black Freedom Riders at a lunch counter in a Montgomery, Alabama, bus station in May 1961. BELOW: Marchers walk from Selma to Montgomery, Alabama, in their campaign for voting rights. FACING PAGE: *African-American Voters*, a painting by Jacob Lawrence.

50s Sporty Cars

"I've always thought that the 1950s stood out more than any other decade in terms of automobile design," says Carl Herrman, whose work on these stamps brought back pleasant memories. "I was in high school and college during the 1950s, so serving as art director on this project was like déjà vu."

To help ensure that others felt that same strong connection with the past, Herrman heeded the suggestion of a Citizens' Stamp Advisory Committee member and selected an artist whose work perfectly defined this era in automotive design: Art "Fitz" Fitzpatrick.

"Fitz is a legend in the world of auto illustration, and he has created more than 1,500 car illustrations," Herrman explains. "The bonus for me was that he lives in Carlsbad, California, just a few miles down the Coast Highway from me. I went to the Newport Beach Concours and found him there, selling his advertising art from the 1950s and '60s."

Before Fitzpatrick became an illustrator, he worked with Howard "Dutch" Darrin in Hollywood, where he helped design custom-built cars for Clark Gable, Errol Flynn, Al Jolson, and other movie stars. As Herrman soon discovered, Fitzpatrick had a knack not only for designing and depicting cars, but also for displaying them in highly flattering contexts.

"Once we had photographs of the cars, Carl and I chose the views that we agreed best portrayed the character of each one," Fitzpatrick explains. "For example, I photographed a mountain snow scene near Bend, Oregon, knowing that it would fit the angle of the photograph of the Studebaker. The scene shows off the wonderful modeling of that front end, along with the red-and-white paint job."

Fondly recalling his memberships in antique car clubs and participation in auto rallies, Herrman could not be happier with the outcome of this project.

"This has been one of most enjoyable projects I've ever worked on," he says. "The final stamp designs look just like Fitz's great auto ads from the 1950s. Each one reflects the touch of a master."

Art "Fitz" Fitzpatrick is a legend in the world of auto illustration, and he has created more than 1,500 car illustrations.

Kaiser Darrin and Nash Healey are trademarks of the DaimlerChrysler Corporation.
Ford and Thunderbird, ™ Ford Motor Company.
General Motors Corvette Trademarks used under license to the USPS.

PLACE AND DATE OF ISSUE
Detroit, MI, August 20, 2005

ART DIRECTOR
Carl T. Herrman

DESIGNER AND ARTIST
Art M. Fitzpatrick

Let's Dance/ Bailemos

The Let's Dance/Bailemos stamps are a truly multi-cultural effort. In addition to being the first bilingual stamps issued in the United States, the designs are the work of four different artists who hail from three different countries: Ecuador, Cuba, and Mexico.

The most critical aspect of this assignment, says Ethel Kessler, the art director and designer for the project, was finding those artists.

"I wanted to use artists who had their own personal associations with each dance," she explains, "but I also needed to choose artists whose work would be compatible. I started with José Ortega; I knew his work, and I knew he loved salsa. Then, as I continued my visual research, I looked for other artists whose work combined the same kind of graphic simplicity combined with layers of pattern."

She adds with a laugh: "But they all had to dance."

For José Ortega, a salsa club owner in Toronto, this project was the perfect opportunity to combine his two loves: art and salsa. Artist Edel Rodriguez created the cha-cha-cha stamp by drawing on memories of his father and sister shuffling to the 1-2, 1-2-3 beat. Sergio Baradat evoked his parents' descriptions of splintering starlight and moonlight filtering through a glass ceiling onto couples spinning to the strains of the Latin big-band sound. For the merengue stamp, artist and dance enthusiast Rafael Lopez brought to bear years of personal experience enjoying this national dance of the Dominican Republic.

None of the four had ever created a stamp design before, but Kessler was confident that their work would be suitable for the format.

"These guys are pros," she says. "The amazing thing was that without any instruction from me they all ended up using essentially the same color palate. Each had a different emphasis; the salsa, for example, is red-hot, but the accent colors are the same as the ones in the mambo. As a result, the designs work fabulously together."

"I wanted to use artists who had their own personal associations with each dance."

PLACE AND DATE OF ISSUE
New York, NY, September 17, 2005

ART DIRECTOR AND DESIGNER
Ethel Kessler

ARTISTS
Edel Rodriguez, Sergio Baradat, Rafael Lopez, José Ortega

Greta Garbo

In 2005, the U.S. Postal Service joins Sweden Post in honoring film legend Greta Garbo. Born in Stockholm in 1905, Garbo received a scholarship to train at the Royal Dramatic Theater Academy. Her work in the epic Swedish film *Saga of Gosta Berling* drew the attention of Louis B. Mayer, production chief of MGM. At his behest, Garbo arrived in the United States with a contract to star in MGM films; she was nineteen.

Carl Herrman, the art director on the project, jumped at the opportunity to design the Garbo stamp. Proud of his own Swedish heritage, he admits he knew little about the screen legend when he started the project, but he found that discovering her life and artistic accomplishments was a delight.

"I have never seen so many beautiful photographs of one woman in my entire career."

"I have never seen so many beautiful photographs of one woman in my entire career," Herrman says. "Initially, I wanted to use an image of her from *Queen Christina*, and I must have watched that movie a dozen times, but in the end I decided the film and the costumes were too historical to work in the stamp format."

Sharing Herrman's concerns, the Postal Service selected a Clarence Bull photograph of Garbo taken during the filming of *As You Desire Me*. A staff photographer for MGM, Bull said that he found Garbo's face "the most inspirational I ever photographed." The designers at Sweden Post loved the image, but they preferred to use an engraving for their stamp design. In October 2004, Sweden Post sent a delegation to share Piotr Naszarkowski's work with their American counterparts.

"When they showed me the engraving I knew instantly that it should be the stamp," says Herrman. "The artwork is as beautiful as she was."

PLACE AND DATE OF ISSUE
New York, NY, and Stockholm, Sweden, September 23, 2005

ART DIRECTOR AND DESIGNER
Carl T. Herrman

ENGRAVER
Piotr Naszarkowski

FACING PAGE: An alluring publicity still of Garbo from the 1930s. ABOVE LEFT: Garbo contends with leading man Antonio Moreno and the domineering Mauritz Stiller in the 1926 film *The Temptress*. ABOVE RIGHT: Garbo in the 1933 film *Queen Christina*.

Constellations

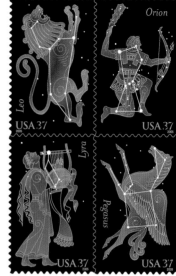

I n its continuing effort to issue stamps that are as educational as they are beautiful, the U.S. Postal Service presents four constellations that light up Northern Hemisphere skies during one of the four seasons. Each design reflects the imaginary lines that we as humans have drawn to connect the stars not only to each other, but also to our own myths, traditions, and everyday lives.

Artist McRay Magleby, who based his illustrations on characters from Greek mythology, found that one of these stamps presented a peculiar challenge of scale.

"Three of the constellations were all roughly the same scale," Magleby explains, "but Lyra, the smallest of the four, is typically only shown as the lyre. To make it work alongside the three other stamps, I found pictures of ancient Greek vases that showed men playing lyres, and then I added Orpheus to the design."

To be sure that the stars were accurately placed for each constellation and that they were shown at the right level of brightness, Magleby used star maps.

To be sure that the stars were accurately placed for each constellation and that they were shown at the right level of brightness, Magleby used star maps by a noted celestial cartographer, a process that raised another interesting issue for the design team.

"We really wrestled with the question of how many stars to show," says art director Carl Herrman. "We debated whether to include only the brightest ones—the ones you can see with the naked eye—or everything you would see if you used a telescope. In the end, we thought it made sense to include only the stars that you can see with your own eyes."

In depicting these formations as our ancestors saw them, Herrman and Magleby remind us that constellations have long served as guideposts for travelers at night, helping astronomers find their way around the heavens—and proving relevant to our lives on earth as well.

LEFT: A detail from a Greek amphora showing a lyre-player. ABOVE RIGHT: The International Astronomical Union recognizes 88 constellations, many of which are associated with Greek mythology. FACING PAGE: A striking illustration from *A Celestial Atlas*, published in 1822.

PLACE AND DATE OF ISSUE
Bloomfield Hills, MI, October 3, 2005

ART DIRECTOR
Carl T. Herrman

DESIGNER AND ARTIST
McRay Magleby

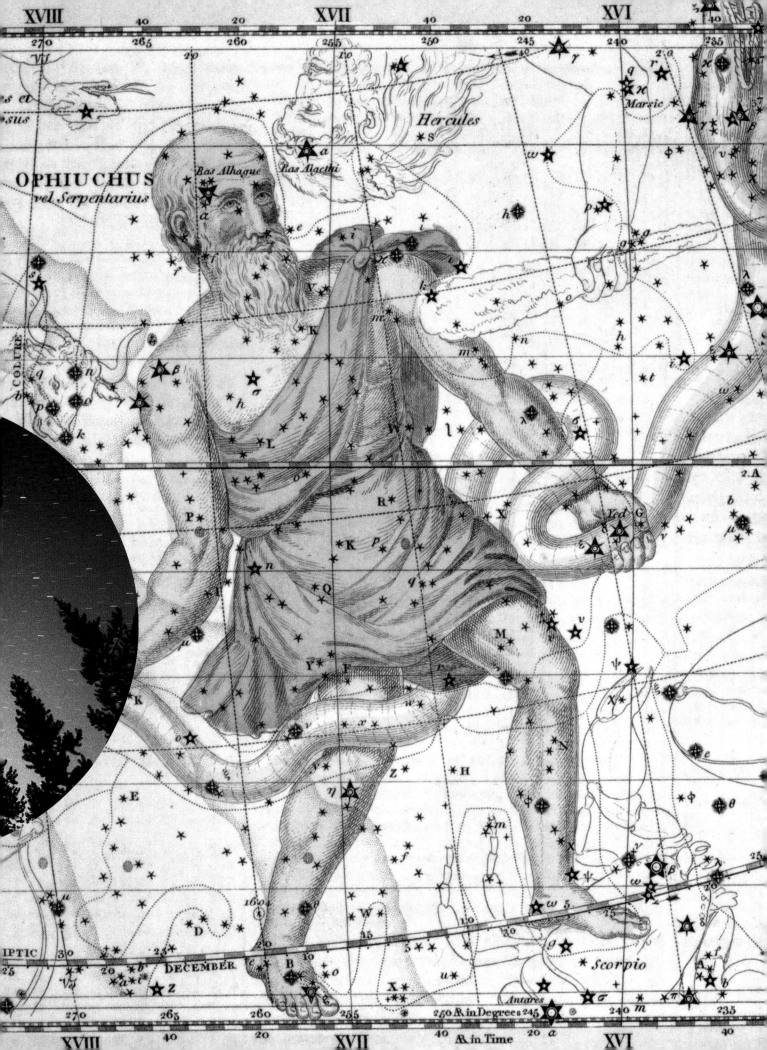

Child Health

With its tender depiction of an iconic scene, the Child Health stamp presents a powerful message. As part of a continued emphasis on increasing awareness of important issues, the Postal Service issues this stamp in 2005 to draw public attention to the active role that parents and caregivers can play in the multifaceted effort to safeguard every child.

"I concentrated on creating something very graphic, symbolic, and universal," says designer Craig Frazier, who focused on the interaction between a child and a doctor. "The image depicts the essential relationship necessary for good child health: a sensitive, nurturing adult—specifically, a doctor—listening closely to the heart of a nervous and attentive child. It is both a literal and metaphorical representation."

To complement the stamp design, selvage text that borders the complete pane draws attention to steps that adults can take to protect the health of children. Some parents and caregivers may be surprised to learn that accidents are the primary cause of death for children in America. Therefore, a major part of children's health care is prevention. Using car seats, "childproofing" the house, and immunizing against disease are all good prevention tools. Those safeguards, combined with the sort of attentive relationship depicted on this stamp, can help ensure that every child receives the best possible start.

"We wanted the stamp to be about more than merely going to the doctor," explains art director Carl Herrman. "We wanted it to be about working with healthcare professionals in a number of areas, about prenatal care, about getting regular medical checkups, and about the importance of regular exercise and good nutrition. We wanted people to know that this was an issue they could do something about."

"I concentrated on creating something very graphic, symbolic, and universal."

PLACE AND DATE OF ISSUE
Philadelphia, PA, September 7, 2005

ART DIRECTOR
Carl T. Herrman

DESIGNER AND ARTIST
Craig Frazier

57

Presidential Libraries

Commemorating the 50th anniversary of the Presidential Libraries Act of 1955, the U.S. Postal Service honors Presidential Libraries and their place in American history with this stamp. Built through private funds and maintained and operated by the National Archives and Records Administration, libraries in the Presidential Library system come into being after a President leaves office, at which point all administration papers fall under the stewardship of the Archivist of the United States.

When veteran stamp designer Howard Paine took on this project, he knew that he would face a challenge: to distill all of the images and information associated with the 12 individual libraries into a single, significant image.

"I started by visiting the individual libraries on the Web," Paine says. "It was an eye-opening journey. I learned that in addition to the President's personal papers, each library includes a fascinating museum that sponsors outreach programs for schools, with interactive videos about that presidency. The more I learned, the more difficult the assignment became."

At first, Paine considered finding something symbolic of the life of each President and the world events that occurred during each administration.

"I tried many solutions," he says, "but they were all too complicated, too busy. I needed something simple and dignified. Then a friend showed me a White House invitation with the Presidential Seal embossed on heavy cream stationery. It made me feel important just to hold it. I knew I had the solution."

Paine further simplified the Seal to show to just the eagle and the stars, and he hired famed calligrapher Julian Waters to do the lettering for the design.

"We knew we couldn't take too many liberties with the Seal," he explains. "The White House jealously guards its use, which is why we were very pleased when they approved of its use on the stamp."

"Each library includes a fascinating museum that sponsors outreach programs for schools, with interactive videos about that presidency."

ABOVE LEFT: The newly refurbished Oval Office awaits the return of President Clinton. ABOVE RIGHT: President Franklin D. Roosevelt speaks during a radio broadcast on November 4, 1938. FACING PAGE: In this 1963 photograph, John Kennedy, Jr., plays under the desk in the Oval Office while President John F. Kennedy works.

PLACE AND DATE OF ISSUE
Abilene, KS, Ann Arbor, MI, Atlanta, GA, Austin, TX, Boston, MA, College Station, TX, Grand Rapids, MI, Hyde Park, NY, Independence, MO, Little Rock, AR, Simi Valley, CA, West Branch, IA, Yorba Linda, CA, August 4, 2005

ART DIRECTOR AND DESIGNER
Howard E. Paine

Holiday Cookies

This year, the U.S. Postal Service celebrates the holiday season with a festive plate of colorful cookies.

"Beautifully decorated sugar cookies capture the magic of the holidays," says photographer Sally Andersen-Bruce. "There's something about the time it takes to create each cookie that makes us remember those special people in our lives and cherish the moment that much more."

For Andersen-Bruce, developing these stamps was a true labor of love. "I must have made hundreds of cookies," she explains. "We treated the good ones with a matte finish so they would hold up under the bright lights. That Santa cookie was probably a year-and-a-half old by the time we finished shooting."

To get the right angle, Andersen-Bruce worked from the top of a six-foot ladder.

"I shot the cookies on white plates, on ivory plates, on silver plates," she says, "and I must have shot half a dozen different doily patterns, too. A local artist, Tommy Simpson, designed the cutters for me. I baked, and then he helped me decorate the cookies."

Two other cookie artists—Emily Diffrient-Crumpton of Austin, Texas, and Rebecca Vermilyea of Bethlehem, Connecticut—also helped with the designs. "Each designer's style of decorating was so distinctive," says Andersen-Bruce. "Each plate was like putting together a small art show."

Art director Derry Noyes praises Andersen-Bruce not only for her dedication, but also for her attention to detail.

"The wonderful thing about working with Sally is that she loves what she does," says Noyes. "Her careful, affectionate approach is evident in every photo."

"Each plate was like putting together a small art show."

PLACE AND DATE OF ISSUE
New York, NY, October 20, 2005

ART DIRECTOR AND DESIGNER
Derry Noyes

PHOTOGRAPHER
Sally Andersen-Bruce

FACING PAGE: The original plate of cookies photographed by Sally Andersen-Bruce is as colorful as it is appetizing.

Credits

Credits

Acknowledgments

These stamps and this stamp-collecting book were produced by Stamp Services, Government Relations, United States Postal Service.

JOHN E. POTTER *Postmaster General, Chief Executive Officer*

RALPH J. MODEN *Senior Vice President, Government Relations and Public Policy*

DAVID E. FAILOR *Executive Director, Stamp Services*

Special thanks are extended to the following individuals for their contributions to the production of this book:

UNITED STATES POSTAL SERVICE

TERRENCE W. McCAFFREY *Manager, Stamp Development*

CINDY L. TACKETT *Manager, Stamp Products and Exhibitions*

SONJA D. EDISON *Project Manager*

HARPERCOLLINS PUBLISHERS

NICK DARRELL *Associate Editor, Collins*

LUCY ALBANESE *Design Director, General Books Group*

SUSAN KOSKO *Director of Production, General Books Group*

JESSICA CHIN *Production Editor, General Books Group*

NIGHT & DAY DESIGN

TIMOTHY SHANER *Art Director, Designer*

PHOTOASSIST, INC.

JEFF SYPECK *Editorial Consultant*

MICHAEL OWENS *Photo Editor, Rights and Permissions*

JENNIFER TRUCANO *Traffic Coordinator*

THE CITIZENS' STAMP ADVISORY COMMITTEE

CARY R. BRICK

MICHAEL R. BROCK

MEREDITH J. DAVIS

DAVID L. ENYON

JEAN PICKER FIRSTENBERG

SYLVIA HARRIS

I. MICHAEL HEYMAN

JOHN M. HOTCHNER

DR. C. DOUGLAS LEWIS

KARL MALDEN

DR. VIRGINIA M. NOELKE

RICHARD F. PHELPS

RONALD A. ROBINSON

MARUCHI SANTANA